I0012076

IPHONE SE 2020 USERGUIDE

Step By Step Guide To Unlock Some Tricks On Your iPhone Se

Smartphone And How To Back Up Your Files On icloud

Without Stress

By

Robert A. Young

Copyright © 2020 Robert A. Young
All rights reserved. No part of this
book shall be reproduced, stored in a
retrieval system, or transmitted by any
means, electronic, mechanical,
photocopying, recording, or
otherwise, without written permission
from the publisher. Although every
precaution has been taken in the
preparation of this book, the publisher
and author assume no responsibility
for errors or omissions. Nor is any
liability assumed for damages
resulting from the use of the
information contained herein.

Table of Contents

CHAPTER ONE

iPhone SE 2020 REVIEW

The iPhone SE (2020) runs on the latest Apple iOS 13.4 operating system and should enjoy approximately 5 years of continuous major and minor software updates. IOS 13 is not a major update to the operating system, rather it focused on improving the default system applications.

Apple iPhone SE Touch ID review

iPhone SE Touch ID biometric security. It's a bit different from the iPhone 8 - press the sensor and the iPhone will unlock as soon as it gets a successful reception. Raising to wake works like a charm, so there is no need to wake up the screen manually.

Lockscreen has three pages:

- center for notifications
- left for today, and
- right for the camera app.

  There is no visible flashlight switch, but you can slide the control center from the bottom and activate it from there.

The navigation gestures are the same as on the iPhone before X: press the Home key for the Home screen / Applications and double-click the task launcher.

The notification center is called up by sliding your finger from the top of the screen. The window is integrated with the lock screen in iOS 11, and if you use different wallpapers for the home and lock screens, you might get confused at first.

Your (customizable) Toggle Control Center slides out from the bottom of the screen. You can use the haptic touch to access additional controls. The battery percentage moves here permanently because there is no space in that status bar.

Notification Center • Control Center

The 3D touch has turned out well and Apple is responsible for its demise. The company seemed to have chosen to ignore it, even though it had many years to use it for more than just prolonged media activism that was largely designed for a quick preview and contextual action pop-ups. Its functionality is still here, but now it just needs to be leveraged instead of a real printer. The Engine provides optimal haptic response and it seems like the 3D touch isn't here yet. We're glad Apple's 3D Touch Layer helped free up space on the phone.

So you can use the haptic touch of various app icons to reveal quick action if available. You can use it to open or expand notifications, toggle, and app content (images, links, file descriptions, etc.). You can use haptic touch to name folders or view remaining notifications.

As usual, a pop-up preview of images, weblinks, messages, emails, notes, and photos is available.

Apple introduced the dark mode of the IS13 system. You can enable it in Display Settings, which changes to dark white backgrounds through iOS. Dark mode affects not only all applications on the system, but also applications that depend on the background of the system. The screen is often in low light, so it saves you some battery life.

You can always choose between active or automatic. The second means that you can program the dark wall manually.

Siri, Apple's digital assistant, is used by more than 400 million people a month. You call it Home Aye Grab. Thanks to all the machine learning improvements, iOS 13 introduces a new voice with an even more natural history.

Siri shortcuts were introduced as part of iOS 12, but now they get their app from shortcuts. There are many things you can assign to a shortcut and it takes many pages to describe them. You can program anything on iOS, a lot on system apps, and any known advanced programs.

CHAPTER TWO

ACCESSORIES FOR IPHONE SE (2020)

You have a new iPhone SE, now what? At the very least, you will need a new case. Since the dimensions of the new iPhone SE are compatible with the iPhone 7 and iPhone 8, the opportunities between these models are interchangeable. One of my all-time favorites is Otterbox's Otter + Pop Symmetry Case because it looks tough, dynamic, and good.

OtterBox Otter + Pop Symmetry Case

Apple iPhone SE silicone case

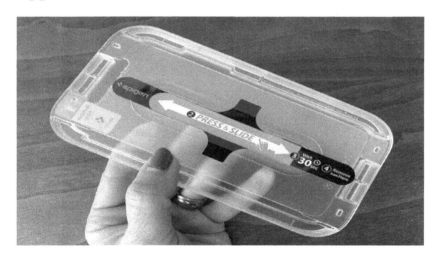

Best screen protector:

Speed tempered glass screen protector

Best wireless charger:

Anchor Powerwave II charging station

Best wireless headphones:

Apple Airpods

Best selfie stick/stand:

Adonit V-Grip

Best fitness almonds: ArmBand

Armored titanium

Best Car Mountain:

Total Wireless Car Charger

Apple watch

CHAPTER THREE

UNBOXING YOUR NEW iPhone SE

When you purchase the new iPhone case, it will be sealed and will be open by you for the first time.

However, you shouldn't accept the product if the seal of the iPhone she was broken.

In this book, I will use a screenshot of three iPhone SE product to show what is inside the new pack of your iPhone

This is how the iPhone Se will look like when it is purchased or delivered to you

Open the phone by first removing the seal

Gently remove the seal

After you open the case of the phone first you will see the little paper use guide

You will also see the sim card opener pin

Also the iPhone paper with the iPhone company logo

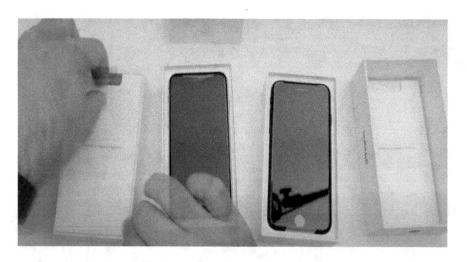

Next, you see your phone

Also, remove the seal from the iPhone SE

This is how the iPhone Se will look like when you first remove it from the pack

Next, you will see the other product that came with your iPhone SE

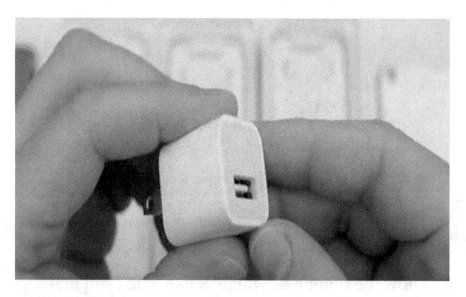

This is the iPhone charger

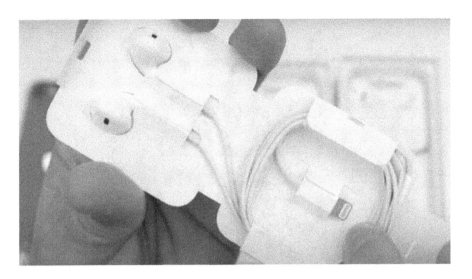

The iPhone SE earpiece

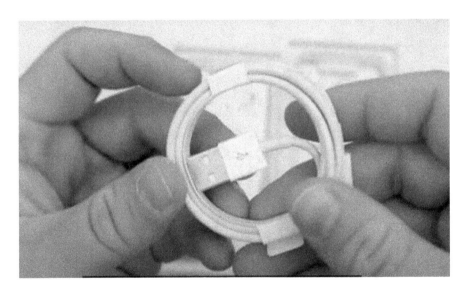

The iPhone SE a charging cable or you can also call it to cord

The iPhone SE sim port

Your iPhone SE

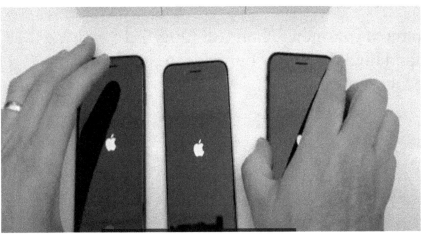

The iPhone logo will display if you fist put on the phone

And now the phone is ready for setup

CHAPTER FOUR

HOW TO SET UP YOUR NEW iPhone SE

1 Deactivate your old phone 1 Deactivate your old phone

2 Turn on your new phone

Welcome to your new iPhone SE (2020). To activate it, press and hold the power button (top right) until the Apple logo appears.

3.Hello

On the "Hello" screen of your phone SE, press the Start button to start the setup.

4 Language and region

Select your language and location (country or region).

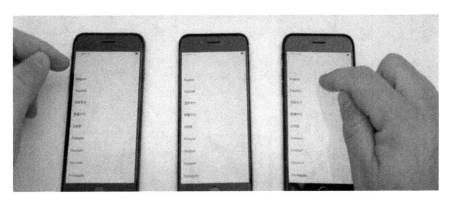

Select language

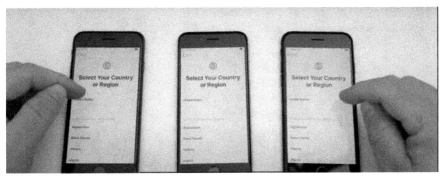

Select your Country or Region

5 Quick start

If your old iPhone has iOS 11 or later, bring your old phone to your new phone now, you will automatically log in and save time!

Touch manual setup to continue.

6.Connect to Wi-Fi Step

Touch the desired Wi-Fi network. Enter the password and tap Join.

7 Activate your new iPhone

If prompted, enter your Verizon PIN. If first time activation doesn't work, press Retry. If you forget it, reset or reset your account PIN.

8 Data and privacy

Apple collects personal information only when you need to activate features, secure your services, or personalize your experience. Press to continue.

9 Touch ID

With this feature, you can use your fingerprints to unlock your phone and make purchases. Touch Continue to follow the instructions or touch Touch ID later.

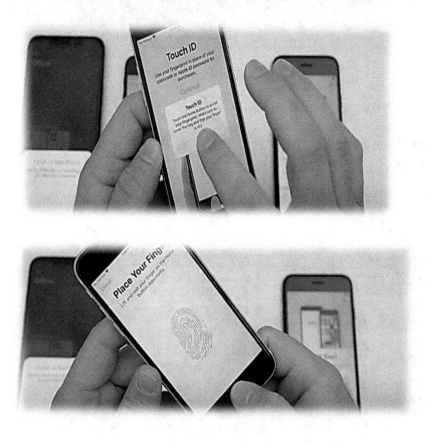

10 Create a password

Here you are required to set up a six-digit passcode to protect your data and other information on your phone. Also, you will need a passcode to use features like Apple Pay, unlock your phone e.t.c. If you don't have a four-digit password, a custom password, or a password, tap Password Options.

11 Restore your phone

Select your backup option. Do you need to transfer content later if the backup is not complete? Choose not to change apps and data.

12 Sign in to your Apple account

Enter your Apple ID and password. This account is used to download new applications to use on your phone and to access any other function such as iCloud.

13 Review Apple's terms and conditions

When you enter your Apple ID, you will be shown the terms and conditions for the review. Review them and tap OK when you're ready.

14 step quick setup

To configure your phone with the recommended settings, tap Continue. If you want to customize any of those options, tap Customize settings.

15. Keep your iPhone up to date

For the latest features, security, and enhancements when updating iOS automatically, tap Continue. Otherwise, tap Install updates manually.

16 Apple Pay

Add cards to Apple Pay to send money to friends and make secure purchases in stores, apps, and the web. To set up Apple Payment, tap Continue. Otherwise, tap on Settings later.

17 Siri

Siri allows you to use your voice to complete various tasks on your device and easily search the web. Touch Continue to set up now or you can set it up later. If you want to set it up now, you will be asked to say a few sentences to identify the voice.

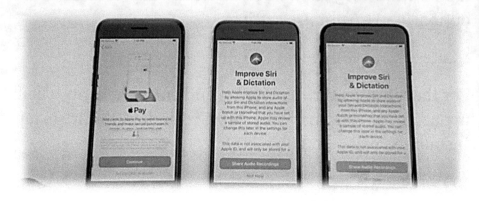

18 screen time

To get weekly reports on your screen time and set timelines for the apps you want to manage, go to Settings or tap Set later.

19 Analysis of the application

Tap on Privacy & App Analytics for more information. If you want to sign up, tap Share with app developers or tap Share.

20.tone display

Adjust the color and intensity of your scene to make images appear more natural. Press to continue.

21 Appearance

Choose a light or dark style for the iPhone, then tap Next.

22 Haptic home button

Select how the first button feels when you press it, then tap Continue (top right).

23 Zoom Show

Choose how you want your iPhone to look, then tap Next.

24 Welcome to iPhone 24

Ready! Touch Get Started to start using your new phone.

it says welcome to iPhone and we're in
so now we're at the home screen and I

CHAPTER FIVE

iPhone SE: A HARDWARE REVIEW

The new iPhone SE has features like the A13 Bionic chip, the fastest chip in a smartphone, and also the best single-camera system in an iPhone

New iPhone SE.

A second-generation iPhone SE with a 4.7-inch Retina HD display, combined with Touch ID for industry-leading security. The iPhone SE has a compact design and has been redesigned from the inside and is the most affordable iPhone. The new iPhone SE is powered by the

A13 Bionic, Apple's fastest-growing smartphone chip. iPhone SE also features one of the best single-camera systems on the iPhone, offering the benefits of computer photography, including portrait mode, and is designed to resist dust and water-resistant elements.

The iPhone SE comes in three beautiful colors: black, white, and (product) red, and pre-orders start at $ 399 (US).

The new second-generation iPhone SE builds on that great idea and improvement in every way, including the best camera system for our best photos and videos, and it remains very much affordable, "this was confirmed by Phil Schiller, Apple's company vice president of Jayce. World Marketing.

iPhone SE in black.

The black front of the iPhone SE features a durable glass and space-grade aluminum design.

Popular design with a 4.7-inch screen

iPhone SE is designed in durable glass and aluminum from the Black Front Space Series and is available in black, white, and (product) red. The rear glass finish features a central Apple logo, which uses a seven-layer color scheme for seven colors and

opacity, giving it rich depth with a strip of matched aluminum. It is water and dust resistant with up to 1 meter for 30 minutes.

The 4.7-inch Retina HD display combines white light with a true-to-life hue to circulating light for a more natural, paper-like viewing experience.

The iPhone SE uses Haptic Touch for quick animations like live photo animation, message preview, application reordering, and more, as well as context menus.

The iPhone SE also has a steel ring to identify the user's fingerprints for the familiar home button and touch identification, which is designed with a bit of sapphire to protect the durability and the sensor. Using Touch ID is an easy, personal, and secure option to enter an iPhone unlock password, enter passwords using the iCloud keyboard, access apps, allow store purchases, and perform Apple payment transactions.

The New iPhone SE Black, White and red colors.

iPhone SE comes in three colors:

1. black
2. white

3. Red

And your iPhone SE is designed to resist and
withstand dust and water.

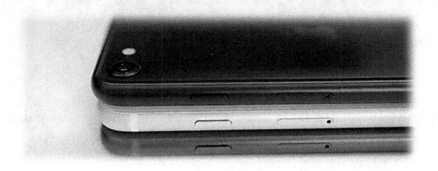

A13 Bionic:

Introduced with the iPhone 11 and iPhone 11 Pro, the A13 Bionic is by far the fastest chip in the smartphone and offers unmatched performance for all the functions that the iPhone SE handles. Perfect for photography, gaming, and experiencing today's reality, the A13 Bionic makes every action feel fluid.

The A13 Bionic is designed with an 8-core neural engine that can run at an estimated speed of 5 trillion per second, two machine learning accelerators in the CPU, with a new machine learning controller to help enhance performance and efficiency. A13 Bionic and iOS 13 together enable machine learning and new smart apps using Core ML.

Built for efficiency, the A13 Bionic offers great battery life for the iPhone SE. iPhone SE comes with a Qi-certified charger that supports fast charging and offers customers a 50 percent charge in as little as 30 minutes. With blazing-fast Wi-Fi 6 and Gigabit LTE-class download speeds available. 3 Dual SIM users with ESIM make it easy to keep two phone numbers separate os on a single device when traveling abroad or as a trade route.

iPhone SE shows the Apple Arcade game.

The A13 Bionic, the fastest chip in the smartphone, comes with the iPhone SE, allowing for longer battery life, power, and efficiency.

New camera experience powered by A13 Bionic

CHAPTER SIX

USE TOUCH ID ON IPHONE

Learn how to set up and use Touch ID, a fingerprint identity sensor that makes your device easy to access.

Set up Touch ID

Use Touch ID

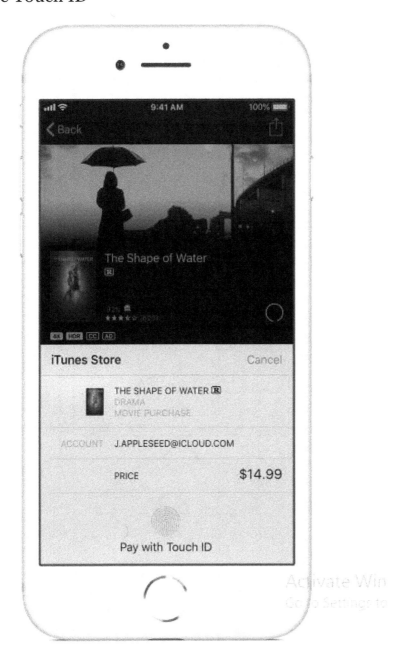

Manage settings

Set up Touch ID

Before setting up Touch ID, you must create a passcode for your device. Then follow these steps:

Start button and make sure your finger is clean and dry.

Touch Settings> Touch ID & password, then enter your password.

Add fingerprints Press and hold the device as usual when you tap the Home button.

Place your finger on the Home button with your finger, but do not press. Hold it until you feel a quick blow or until you are asked to lift your finger.

Raise your finger slowly and relax, always making small changes to the position of your finger.

The next screen instruction will notify you to adjust your grip. Press and hold the device as usual when unlocking it and tap the Home button with the outer area within arm's reach instead of the central part that you originally scanned.

Note:

If inserting a finger is difficult, try another finger.

CHAPTER SEVEN

APPLE IPHONE SE CONTROL CENTER

The Control Center provides quick access to many settings and functions

1. Swipe up gently from the bottom of the screen

2.

2. On the network card, you can touch an icon to enable and disable airplane mode and mobile data, as well as disconnect from Bluetooth devices and Wi-Fi networks.

3. The audio card allows you to control the audio that is currently playing.

4. You can change the brightness and volume by dragging the slider up and down

5. Tapping an icon opens an application or enables or disables a function

6. You can see additional options for some icons by tapping and holding an icon

7 From the home screen, tap Settings to customize the Control Center

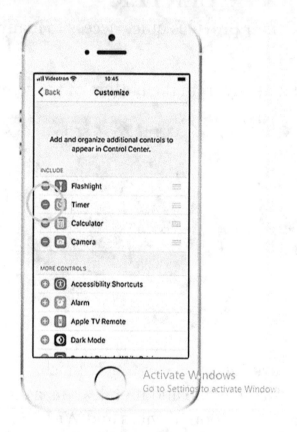

8.Scroll down and tap Control Center

9.Tap Custom controls

10. To delete a control, tap the Delete icon next to it

Tap to delete

12. To add a control, tap the icon next to it

13. To rearrange the order of the icons, tap and hold the three rows next to the icon

14. Drag it into place and lift your finger

15. Touch the back arrow to save your selections

The notification center is called up by sliding your finger from the top of the screen. The window is integrated with the lock screen in iOS 11, and if you use different wallpapers for the home and lock screens, you might get confused at first.

Your (customizable) Toggle Control Center slides out from the bottom of the screen. You can use the haptic touch to access additional controls. The battery percentage moves here permanently because there is no space in that status bar.

Notification Center • Control Center

The 3D touch has turned out well and Apple is responsible for its demise. The company seemed to have chosen to ignore it, even though it had many years to use it for more than just prolonged media activism that was largely designed for a quick preview and contextual action pop-ups. Its functionality is still here, but now it just needs to be leveraged instead of a real printer. The Taptic Engine provides optimal haptic response and it seems like the 3D touch isn't here yet. We're glad Apple's 3D Touch Layer helped free up space on the phone. So you can use the haptic touch of various app icons to reveal quick action if available. You can use it to open or expand notifications, toggle, and app content (images, links, file descriptions, etc.). You can use haptic touch to name folders or view remaining notifications.

As usual, a pop-up preview of images, weblinks, messages, emails, notes, and photos is available.

CHAPTER EIGHT

BATTERY LIFE AND CHARGING

The iPhone SE (2020) runs on a 1,821 mAh battery, the capacity of the iPhone 8, although it is a different cell. You can charge iPhone SE with your old 5W charger, your 18W Pro charger, or any USB-PD charger. The iPhone SE also supports wireless charging, making it an option.

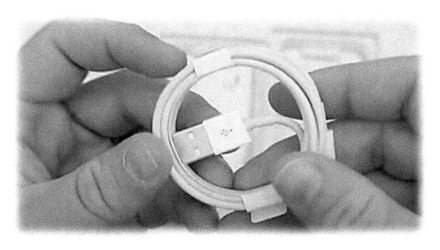

The iPhone SE comes with a standard 5V / 1A charger that charges 27% of the shipped battery in 30 minutes and takes 2 hours and 30 minutes to fully charge.

The iPhone SE scored high during our battery test: it can last up to 10 hours of 3G calls, and 13 hours of web browsing with a single charge, or it can watch up to 9 hours of video. Good but noticeable overall endurance rating is 59 hours as endurance is above average.

However, for such a small battery, the runtimes on the screen were quite respectable.

CHAPTER NINE

HOW TO USE AIRDROP ON YOUR IPHONE SE

You can use AirDrop to share and receive images, documents, and more with other nearby Apple devices.

Before you start

Make sure the person you are sending is close to and in a range of Bluetooth and Wi-Fi.

Check if you and the sender have Wi-Fi and Bluetooth enabled. If you both have a private hotspot enabled, disable it.

Check if the sender is set to receive only from your AirDrop contacts. If they do and you are in contact with them, they will need your email address or mobile phone number on your contact card for AirDrop to work.

If it's not in your contacts, set your AirDrop Receipt settings so that each of them receives the file.

To control who can see your device and who can send you Content in AirDrop, you can remove the AirDrop Receipt setting from Contacts Only or Receipt.

How to use AirDrop

Open the app, tap the Share or Share button. If you share a photo from the Photos application, you can slide your finger left or right to select multiple photos.

Touch the AirDrop user you want to share.

Note:

If you can't see the AirDrop user or your other Apple device? Learn what to do.

If the person you are sharing with us in your contacts, you will see a picture with their name. If they are not in your contacts, you will only see their name without an image.

How to accept AirDrop

If someone shares something with you using the AirDrop feature, you will see an alert with a preview. You can either touch Accept or Decline.

If you tap OK, AirDrop will appear in the app that sent it. For example, photos appear in the Photos app and on websites opened in Safari. You can download or purchase the application as it opens in the online App Store.

If you drop something like a photo from your iPhone to Mac, you have no choice but to accept or reject it; it will be sent automatically to your device. Make sure both devices are connected with the same Apple ID.

How to configure AirDrop settings

To choose who can see your device and send you AirDrop content:

Go to Settings, tap General.

Tap AirDrop and then select an option.

In Control Center you can configure AirDrop options. That's how:

- Press and hold the Network Settings in the upper left corner of your phone.
- Press and hold the AirDrop button, then select one of these options:

Receipt: You will not receive AirDrop requests.

Contacts only - Your device will only be visible to your contacts.

Everyone - Your device is visible to all nearby Apple devices that use AirDrop.

If you see a receipt and can't touch to change it:

Go to Settings> Screen Time.

Tap Content and privacy limits.

Tap Permissions and make sure AirDrop is enabled.

CHAPTER TEN

iPhone SE LOCK FOR PERFECT FOCUS

The AE / AF lock feature is priceless to get the perfect iPhone focus and exposure in your photos. If you are wondering how to access this feature and why you want to use it, this article has the answers! In this tutorial, you will learn how to enable AE / AF lock on your iPhone camera and how to use it during various shooting situations. Once you've mastered AE / AF lock, you can be sure your photos will always be sharp with perfect exposure.

AE is an automatic exposure. Exposure is the brightness of the image. AF is autofocus. The focus is on where the image is clearly in focus.

AEAF lock

If you point your iPhone's camera at a scene and press the shutter button, the camera will decide where in the scene (usually the center of the frame) to focus.

The camera must focus on the subject you are trying to create to create the maximum possible image. So instead of letting the iPhone decide what to focus on, you should always manually adjust the focus.

AEAF lock

To set the focal point, you can tap once on the iPhone screen. Doing this will also adjust the exposure level (how bright the subject is). The camera aims to ensure that the target area is correctly exposed (neither too bright nor too dark).

When you tap to focus, a yellow frame will appear around the part of the scene you are touching. This indicates where you are focusing. If you want to adjust the exposure to lighten or darken the image, slide your finger up or down on the screen.

AEAF lock

A single tap to focus works well in most cases, but in some cases, this may not be enough. For example, if something moves in the scene, the camera's auto-centering system can be activated and the focal point and exposure level can be reset automatically.

To make sure this does not happen, you can use the AE / AF lock function to lock the focus and exposure values. This automatically disables the focus system and allows you to control focus and exposure.

How to use AE / AF lock for focus and exposure

To lock the focus and exposure point, touch that part of the screen and hold it down for a few seconds. When you see the AE / AF lock in the yellow frame at the top of the screen, release your finger.

The exposure level is automatically adjusted to correctly expose the area you are focusing on, just as you would with a single touch. However, you can still change the exposure by pushing it up or down on the screen.

To unlock focus and exposure, tap anywhere on the screen. The AE/AF lock of your iPhone SE in the yellow frame will disappear to show that you no longer have the focus and exposure lock anymore.

Once you are in focus, it is important to note that the distance between your camera and the subject should not change. In other words, don't stray from your subject.

If you move forward or backward, the camera focuses on the wrong part of the scene.

The flowers are shown below in the foreground and the background appears blurry.

AEAF lock

Therefore, once you activate the AE / AF lock, do not move the camera closer or closer to the subject.

To go forward or backward to reset your shooting, tap once on the screen to deactivate AE / AF lock, then reset the focus and exposure from your new shooting location.

When to use AE / AF lock?

The AE / AF lock function is useful in most shooting situations. You can get in the habit of wearing it every time you take a photo.

Let's take a look at some common cases where AE / AF lock is used to help you get better focus and exposure in your image.

1. Any scene that moves in the background

If your vision includes moving elements in the background, your iPhone may be tricked into focusing on this element of the scene.

Huge focus.

For example, if a person or a vehicle is moving behind your subject, the camera can point to that moving subject.

AEAF lock

Using AE / AF Lock will prevent this from happening and allow you to focus on your main subject. Once the focus is locked and enabled, the camera will

CHAPTER ELEVEN

HOW TO RECORD THE SCREEN OF YOUR APPLE 2020

Recording a video with audio on the screen of your mobile/mobile phone can be very useful for a tutorial or to show someone who knows how to perform certain tasks on the Apple iPhone SE (2020). File it and send it or upload it to a platform like YouTube or social networks.

Sometimes we like to record a video of an acquaintance, a phone call, or a video call (face to face) with a family member on Instagram or use it as a test or as tic-tac-toe. Video.

Follow these steps to make this recording on your Apple iPhone SE (2020):

1- First step:

First of all, we must make sure that we have screen recording control on our iPhone SE (2020) (we can go to 2nd place if we already have it) to "customize the controls", we look for "Screen registration", lower left red If a token appears we have already enabled it, otherwise click the green + icon and click add dashboard panel.

2- Step 2:

(iPhone 7 and earlier and iPad iOS 11 or earlier) Swipe up and down from the screen where you want to start the video. (iPhone X, iPad with iPad 12 or iPad) Swipe down from the upper right corner of the screen where you want to start the video.

3- Step 3:

If you want to record a video on your Apple iPhone SE (2020) without using a microphone, press the record icon, it will start counting in 3 seconds and then the recording will begin, you will see a red line at the top of the screen and "Record" The word "do" implies that everything that happens on the screen is recorded.

If you want to record a video using the microphone in addition to the iPhone SE (2020) and sound (for example, it is useful to explain the functionality of an application or to record a message while recording a video. Click the Apple iPhone screen button SE (2020)) Press and hold the on-screen icon on the microphone and enable or disable it for 3 seconds and recording will start.

4- Step 4:

To stop recording, you need to open the Control Center (second in this tutorial) and click the Stop Recording button or click the red line in the status bar at the top of the screen of your iPhone SE device and click " Stop".

5- Step 5:

To view and share the screen video recording on your Apple iPhone SE (2020), go to the Photos app, where you can find it last.

On your iPhone SE (2020) you can record video thanks to its internal RAM of 64GB 3GB, 128GB 3GB RAM, 256GB 3GB RAM.

CHAPTER TWELVE

iPhone SE CAMERA

Released in April 2020, the iPhone SE (2020) is an update to Apple's small, cheap and popular SE smartphone. Although it is slightly larger and heavier than the original SE, it is inferior to most newer IPS-powered smartphones with a 4.7-inch LCD screen and a resolution of 1334 × 750 pixels.

However, it's not lacking in power thanks to Apple's latest A13 bionic chip; The new iPhone SE is available with a fixed storage capacity of 64/128 / 256GB

Testing the rear camera of the Apple iPhone SE (2020)

The rear camera for photography offers a single 12MP camera with an f / 1.8 aperture lens. The lens contains PDAF autofocus and Optical Image Stabilization (OIS).

The single-camera setup means that the iPhone SE5x is a portrait model with digital magnification and "advanced bokeh and depth control", although it does not have an extremely wide camera, with bokeh or zoom. Other features include a true-tone LED flash with slow sync and red-eye correction, six-effect lighting control, smart HDR, and JPEG settings, as well as Apple's HEIF image format to save space.

For video, the device can capture 4K at 24/30 / 60fps, as well as provide 1080p slo-mo views at 120 or 240fps. The HDR setting can capture video up to 30fps, and you can get 8K still images while recording 4K video or get timely videos with stabilization. Video formats include HEVC and H.264.

Main Camera Specifications:

Single-camera device

12MP sensor

F / 1.8 aperture lens

PDAF autofocus

Visual image stabilization

5x digital magnification

HEIF and JPEG formats

CHAPTER THIRTEEN

TURN ON TWO-FACTOR AUTHENTIFICATION IN SETTINGS

If your device is using iOS 10.3 or later version:

Go to Settings> tap Password and security on your device.

Touch to enable two-factor authentication.

Press to continue.

If you are using a device with iOS 10.2 or earlier version:

Go to Settings> iCloud.

Tap your Apple ID> Password & security.

Touch to enable two-factor authentication.

Press to continue.

You will be asked to answer the security questions for your Apple ID.

Enter your trusted phone number and verify

Enter the phone number required to receive verification codes when you log in. You can choose to receive codes via SMS or automated phone call.

The next time you tap, Apple will send a verification code to the phone number you provided.

To verify your phone number, enter the verification code, and enable two-factor authentication.

Enable two-factor authentication on your Mac

If you use macOS Catalina:

From the Apple menu, select System> System Preferences, then click Apple ID.

Click Password and Security under your name.

Click Enable Two-Factor Authentication.

If you use Makos Moja or before:

From the Apple menu, select System> System Preferences, then click iCloud and select Account Details.

Click on Security.

Click Enable Two-Factor Authentication.

Steps on how to create an Apple ID on the website.

If you have an Apple ID that is not protected by two-factor authentication, some Apple websites may ask you to update your account.

What to keep in mind when using two-factor authentication

Two-factor authentication help to improve the security of your Apple ID. After enabling it, you will need your password and access to your trusted devices or phone numbers to log into your account. To keep your account as secure as possible and make sure you never lose access, here are some simple guidelines to follow:

Remember your Apple ID password.

You can use a device passcode on all your iPhone SE device.

You can keep your trusted phone number up to date on your iPhone device.

Keep your trusted devices physically safe.

Manage your account

Manage your trusted phone numbers, trusted devices, with other information from your Apple ID account page.

How to keep your trusted phone numbers up to date on your iPhone se Consider verifying a reliable phone number other than yours. If your iPhone is your only trusted device and it is lost or damaged, you will not receive the necessary verification codes to access your account.

If you want to update trusted phone numbers follow these steps:

Go to your Apple ID account page.

Sign in with your Apple ID.

Go to the Security section, select Edit.

If you wish to add a phone number, You can click Add a trusted phone number and enter the correct phone number. Select to verify the number with an SMS or automated phone call and click Continue. If you want to remove a trusted phone number from your device, click the x icon next to the phone number you want to remove.

View and manage your trusted devices

You can view and manage your list of trusted devices in the Devices section of your iOS, macOS, and your Apple ID account page. On iOS:

Go to Settings> [Your name].

Select a device from the list.

In macOS Catalina:

Apple menu Select System> System Preferences.

Select Apple ID.

Select a device from the sidebar.

On or before Makos Moja:

Apple menu Select System> System Preferences.

Select iCloud and then click Account Details.

Click on the Devices tab.

Select a device from the list.

In the net:

Go to your Apple ID account page.

Sign in with your Apple ID.

Go to the Devices section.

Displays the list of devices that you are currently signed in with your Apple ID. Select a device to view device information, such as format and serial number. Below you will find other useful information, including whether the device is trustworthy or not, that you can use to receive Apple ID verification codes.

You can remove a trusted device by selecting Remove from the account on the device list.

Note:

To delete or remove a trusted phone number from your device is such that it will no longer display and show verification codes and blocks access to iCloud and other Apple services on the device until you sign in again with two-factor authentication. If you want to find or remove your device before removing it from your trusted device list, you can use Find My iPhone.

Generate application-specific passwords

With two-factor authentication, provided by third-party apps or Apple

www.ingramcontent.com/pod-product-compliance
Lightning Source LLC
LaVergne TN
LVHW051613050326
832903LV00033B/4484